TAMESIS

A COLLECTION OF RIVERSIDE VERSE

EDMUND HALL

Foreword by
IAN MCKELLEN

To Sarah,

Thank you for your support!

Ed

Chiselbury

Edmund Hall

Published by Chiselbury Publishing, a division of Woodstock Leasor Limited, 14 Devonia Road, London N1 8JH, United Kingdom

www.chiselbury.com

ISBN: 978-1-917837-24-8 (hardback)
ISBN: 978-1-917837-25-5 (epub)
A CIP catalogue record for this book is available from the British Library

Cover design and illustrations by Gary Partridge

Contents

Foreword

For more than 40 years I've lived overlooking the Thames, downstream of the old Port of London. I'm not surprised that others have been inspired to paint the changing tides and to describe them too in words.

Ed Hall's poems are intensely personal, written about his time spent on and by the River Thames. They record high drama alongside wistful reverie, all linked by his unsentimental love of the ancient waterway.

The words are simple that describe the graphic scenes and events, he has observed and been part of. They merit being spoken out loud. The river lives through sights and sounds even as it embraces death.

I commend them to you, these lines that Armitage would be proud of, or Betjeman too.

Ian McKellen
Limehouse Reach
2025

Introduction

It's cold tonight.

Bitterly cold. And bloody wet.

I suspect that many friends are at home in front of warming fires around me here in West London, or tucked up in front of a movie, or maybe even meeting in a pub for a pint of proper ale.

I'd love to be doing that too, but tonight, I'm not, because it's one of my two shifts a month as a volunteer on the crew of the RNLI lifeboat at Chiswick. For someone as active and busy as I am, my time spent here for more than two decades is a grounding reality check. I've spent days travelling and working all over the world in my day job, but then a calendar reminder pops up on my phone, and it's time to go and do what my heart has always wanted to do: to spend time on the lifeboat standing by, and maybe, just occasionally, to have the chance to help save a life.

And so, as I think about writing this, I'm wrapped in warm layers of yellow waterproofs, and checking lights, and radios, and diesel engines and a pair of high-powered water jets.

It's a privilege to serve on a lifeboat crew, and even when it's so bone-numbingly cold, like it is tonight, I know I'm doing something real, something good, something that helps me know I'm not just a random name who does something in *consultancy*, whatever that is.

Maybe that's part of why I'm here? Maybe it proves I'm real?

Standing on the lifeboat at night, looking down the river past Chiswick Ait to Hammersmith, has always asked other questions of me. Even in the heart of London, you breathe in the ancient truths and legends about this river. The names we learn for our local knowledge tell a story older than my time here: Oliver's Island, Syon Reach, Sheen Gulls, Imperial Wharf and the River Wandle. These aren't just place names on a training chart, they could be copied from an index in a history of London, or a history of Londoners, or simply of mankind. This river is part of our common family tree, and I'm privileged to have spent so many years volunteering on it.

For much of my time here, I've also lived much further inland at the other end of the Thames, where the river disappears around wooded bends, and where you can escape from any sign of human life. I stood in 2007 with other West Oxfordshire locals, watching terrible floods rip the walls away from the old stone bridge that took me to the railway station in Charlbury, and as I found my eyes following the foaming polluted brown water heading down river, I wondered how long it would take to reach the lifeboat station at Chiswick. These places are connected.

Long riverside walks and old books have kept me awake dreaming about the history and geography of the river, and my writing is inspired by the words of many others before me, caught by a similar riverine spell.

I find myself looking for lines, or contrarian thoughts, or images that jar, and when I do, I often scribble them down and send them to myself. Days, weeks or even months later, I find them again, and that's usually when the poems start to form. Frequently, my inspiration dies, and the lines stay there, waiting for another view, or thought, or dream to kick them back to life. *Chiswick Reach* took me ten years to shape, and I hope it tells a story of the river I have spent so many hours working on, searching for casualties, or simply patrolling at a leisurely six knots, looking around and thinking about the history and nature that surrounds me. *Waterloo Sunset* came to life when I was sitting and just looking at Waterloo bridge from the lifeboat station next door and half-remembering my mother's words.

I've tried to capture the river, and the lifeboat, and some of the very random experiences I have had on this incredible winding line of history from Oxford to Gravesend. I hope that some of the poems help to bring you with me, to see what I see, to have a glimpse into my imagination, and to fall in love with the river that so many people forget is the real beating heart of London.

Our boat checks are done now, our bright orange Thames lifeboat is bumping sharply against the pontoon as the wash from a passenger boat lifts her up and drops her down, stretching the lines that hold her. We're heading up to the lifeboat station now to make some tea and dry ourselves out, and have a good old gossip, and stand by for our very loud red telephone to ring.

Whilst we wait, I hope you have a chance to read the poems that have given me something to think about over my many years waiting for action, just like we are now.

1
On Watch

At night, the bright lights fight
To catch the eye, and then reflect
And catch again, and disappear behind,
Is that another boat? Not sure if I am right.

The busy paths are full of selfie lights
And giant screens that dominate
With theatre ads and laser shows, tonight
The river hides in darkness, lost to sight.

The strolling laughter, unaware that feet below
A choppy dirty tidal flow
Is swishing, swooshing, slamming boats
Against their piles and causing creaks of mooring lines.

A *boom boom boom* echoes in rhymes:
A party boat with dancing multi-coloured guests
Slides by, with no idea that just outside
An ink black river passes; working craft of every size.

We sit, and watch, make cups of tea,
And wonder what will ring the bell.
A tourist fall, a broken knee,
Or worse, a suicide attempt.

In yellow here, but up and down the tidal town
Are others waiting: black and orange, green and red,
For other bells, and bleeps and maydays on the VHF
To launch us all, to stop another victim drown.

A river disco ends, an evening stroll is done.
The party's over; people headed home
Glance down from high-bridged pavements, unaware
That looking back are volunteers,
Who turn and put the kettle on.

2
Chiswick Reach

Fast-moving, smooth and mud-shit-brown; the polished
surface dots with
Silver flecks of insects that lived their whole life in a day.
The water flows uphill to Richmond here, deceiving
those who think the Thames
Is just a river headed down from Oxford to the sea.

Harsh-bright morning light caught as dazzling liquid
sparks that drown,
And diverse shades of every green from hornbeam
white to London plane.
Great reaches here that seem as far away from town or
gown
As sleepy oxbows on the Trent, or secret Devon
estuaries that once hid World War games.

Yet, here, too, once mighty kings rowed past, or once
were rowed
By teams of watermen, all liveried to their family's
trade.
They rode the tides from Richmond, Syon, Chiswick
House and down and down
All muscles fighting as they strained,
Each panting hard, like muscled Oxbridge boys and
girls today,
To find the fastest line and curve and
And beat another Royal barge away, away.

Each double-mile here, Tudor-stockinged wealth ate
 ugly river fish in fuck-you palaces,
Carved stone from quarries far away, barged here to
 jetties long-now-lost beneath a new Elizabethan
 realm.
New roads might hide, but also show, the lines of fords
 where Vikings, Celts and Angles
Found ways to wade across, to buy a bale of Cotswold
 wool or Roman valley corn.

A working flowing sludge, each palace river-gate a door
To hide the stinking crap and piss that flowed from
 every town and house ashore.
A foul and vital artery, with ferries, tanneries and more.
Ragged mudlarks tearing penny-lives from selling dog
 turds gathered on the shore.

Here jostled campshed wharves and mad-high-crate-
 piled docks,
And money men in sheds that paid for diverse lighters,
 spreets and yawls
All fight for space and tide and wind to trade their hay
For dung or bricks, and drop their bargee masts and
 duck beneath an iron bridge.

Crews ride tides out, ignore an ancient tower where
 once a marble general ruled for Rome.

In later years, the truth of words for dock and wharf in
 deco fonts was masterly re-spun
In well-bound brochures that promise both an otter's
 splash and lifestyle fun.

With gyms that never close and new craft pubs, with
two-for-one
On weekdays, meant for towpath pensioners in search
of freedom and some lunch.

Not once in all those years, have daily tides refused to
come or go.
Alongside concrete ships with something made in
Germany of chrome or stainless steel,
Highlighting a river-view; or bleached hardwoods, or
chefs in search of stars who know
That here is something new, deserving of a Thames-
themed lunchtime deal.

The barges stay, smart-wanted now, excluding genes of
ancient river folk,
Whose rusted bikes don't neatly fold and lock beside a
gas-fired grill.
Some paint a watering can with floral curls, that may be
true, but as a project now,
Copied from a YouTube film, not taught by hand from
parents moored at Kew.

A tourist river viewed from safe on board a passing
pleasure boat,
Annoying tannoy-echoed commentary of lives lived
here or there or not at all, in Cockney;
Heard with laughter knowing that the truth of them is
not the point.
It is the spirit of the Thames they want, not sterile
truths to sour pints of ale.

This is a city's heart baptised in drink, with brick-built
towers brewing pale

From yeasts as old as time in barrels at the Lamb, and
Stag and even Young's, until the
Rich new young arrived. They built a thousand
stripped-back lofts
Where high-end Pilsner bottles line Sub-Zero fridges,
relegating London's river ale.

A playground too, for grown-ups now; not as it was for
Thirties' lads in black and white.
They paddle board, or sail or swim, or join a swanky
club to row
And differentiate, by class, the working Thames from
ladies in the eights
who watch their waists and listen to a cox call, "Go!"

And when I drift or motor by, and see my City with a
sailor's eye
It is a different view, so quickly lost to rules of north and
south and up and down
Because the river won't be told, and suddenly an open
reach is curling back, and that is why,
that aircraft heading west seem not to be, until you
think and point, and frown.

The view for most, of water from the bridge is worth a
moment's stop and stare,
But not for all, because for some this is the time and
moment, standing there
That they have come to reach the end of dreams, and
lives, and hopes laid bare
And weighted down with life, or iron, they make that
final step into the air.

The tides release by death is old as man's life here.
    Pirates shackled for a flooding tide.
A traitor's barge. A final ride to those condemned by
    kings and queens.
More than a vein perhaps, a thousand pints of human
    blood course through it,
Put there by man in war, and peace, and countless
    accidents unseen.

A parrot flying by, more properly a parakeet apparently
    (though nobody knows why)
Another new invader, sitting now in trees on aits and
    docks where Cromwell hid
Alongside grey, tall-necked herons that hold a stare
    more puritan:
A bird to ban ice fairs, perhaps, not like the bright green
    birds from far away.

3
Thames Valley Blue

Beneath a warm indulgent-blue Cretaceous sky, a
thousand million molluscs die
In shallow seas. A giant long-necked creature wades,
and falls, deep-gouged by teeth,
And sinks beneath the waves, an ancient body slowly
rotting here: beneath primeval mud to lie
Unseen for almost countless years, as yet unnamed; a
stony challenge to belief.

A million million nameless creatures more, laid bodies
thick; our ocean's floor.
Pangea torn unheard as newly-minted continents
collide, and epochs pass: a meterorite.
And over here, a sea retreats, the North of Wales, and
maybe more.
And Cumbria, the proud Cairngorms, and later on, the
Yorkshire Moors.

No man has yet set foot, or even seen our Thames, but
she is forming, running here
From Snowdon down and round what would become
the valley towns,
And turns back north, to where she meets our sea,
along a beach that runs quite clear
From Amsterdam around the warm and marshy land to
Hunstanton, or Brancaster.

No London yet, no Romans here, nor barely mammals
yet to fight, to win the prize
From dinosaurs, whose time has come. And as it rains,
a modern valley forms,
The Medway, Colne and Kennet too, becoming one.
Creating life.
The tropics, heat, and countless trees, the heart of Eden
rising from the storms.

So was it here, just west of Slough, that Eve reached up,
and took a bite,
And covered up, to Adam's shame?
Was England's Green and Pleasant land, a riverside,
An apple's throw from Birmingham?

4
Resuscitation

I remember the shared look:
We knew he wasn't coming back.
Bruised knees and tired arms,
Shoulders aching, adrenaline draining.
For nearly 30-minutes, taking turns,
We crossed our hands and found the spot
To lean and press our cold hands firmly down.

A wet and heavy man, in denim:
We found him on the river's bed,
Never knowing if he jumped or walked
Into the river. But as the tide receded,
Our crew was called, a lifeboat needed.

At first, it seemed so obvious that life had gone,
But as I pressed my thumb against his forehead
In the early morning sun, his blood returned, and so I said,
We have a life sign here, it's time to run.

We looked around and understood
That on a rising tide was not the place
To start our cardiac compression.
The three of us took hold and lifted him
Up to the shore where concrete made a better place
To try our bloody best to bring him back.

Edmund Hall

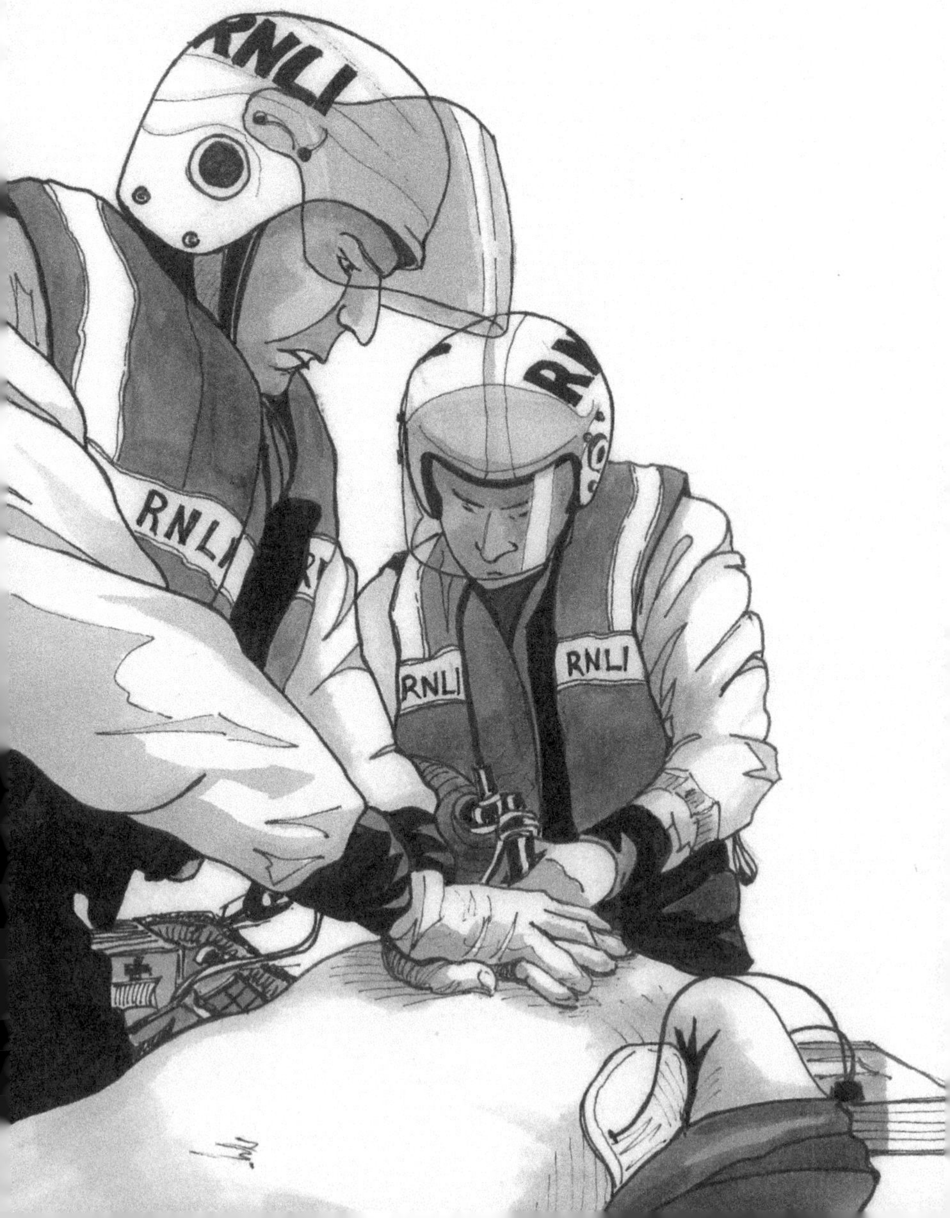

A square red bag, a message sent:
A pair of sticky pads, a silent chest that's clammy white.
A call for real help in green and yellow,
And then that day,
When it's just you,
That has to find a way to stop
A life you never knew
Slipping silently away.

Later, when the doors have closed,
An ambulance drives slowly up the river side.
Their journey now: a hearse, a stately pace.
The litter of first aid blows silently across the road,
And we pretend it's just a job,
Shake hands and say how hard we tried.

5
Barn Elms Reach

A rose-skied sunset over Craven Cottage.
A still and mirrored tide.
An air of expectation dances on the surface,
As walkers stride on the other side.

A wait that's worth its weight.
A twilight with a prize.
A view that's quickly changing,
A river melts to trick the eye.

At once, and suddenly,
All windows here reflect deep polished gold.
A river that was water, glistering.
All movement stops for young and old,
A rower holds.
And here we stop and stare:

A shared and treasured sight.
A seven-minute wonder of the world,
A gleaming river suddenly worth billions,
A molten golden metal stream reflects,
A world of other-worldly light.

A few short precious moments.
A sunset, and a swift return, aureum gone.
A normal river view is back,
A glimpse from cycle paths and dirty windows,
A busy urban river now.
A sculler starts again.

Edmund Hall

6
Sonning

A mason's bridge brings fortune to the shore
With coaching inns, and bones of saints to see.
The pilgrims pay the ferryman no more,
And cross on foot, delighted that it's free.

Before the train and lock and the M4,
This was a vital place to disembark,
A service station, wenches, ales and more
Between the city's castles and a bishopric.

Kingfishers hunt, flash suddenly electric blue
And traffic lights, reversing cars that flow
In alternate directions, pausing to
Allow a second glance and chance to know

That Sonning's hidden brown trout pools reflect,
An ancient village, worthy of a sonnet

Edmund Hall

7
Beverley Brook

I ask myself, where does a river start?
In hills and wolds? Or is it in the heart?
And is this stream a part
Of any grand design?
God's work of art?
Or is it just a sign,
A quirk of old geography
Riparian, that has to find
A way to wind behind
This secret tributary?

8
Composed on Westminster Bridge

September 3, 2022

For centuries, the centre of the world!
A view less fair: a bit industrial,
Our parliament, an ancient hospital,
And palaces: union flags unfurled!
Tourist voices, strange accents to be heard,
Hold camera phones, their memories full.
Protesters in orange to Just Stop Oil
Wave angry banners, as they're uncurled.
Red buses cross, and river boats which show
A thousand ways to register a view
That captivates: for those that know
The long hand means that shortly you
Will hear the Big Ben bells from here below!

OIL

9
Night Watch Blues

Communications overload.
My brain is launched on service.
Battersea Bridge, threatening to jump.
A woman, passers-by, an ambulance.

Standing on the shore
A dark red herring walks away.
Marine Police. A crackly radio, a mouth that cannot find a microphone.
I hush the crew and listen hard.

A moment's rest, our helmets off.

A person calling, stuck in mud, a rising tide.
We cannot find the place in Chiswick Reach.
Blue lights above, and on the shore
A helicopter, searchlights, more and
More police. The fire brigade.
An ambulance commander
Arrives, asking me daft questions, overtalking
Vital calls from hi-tech eyes up in the sky.

A fruitless search, we look again,
A phone's small torch attracts our eyes.
Behind the ait, too shallow, where
We cannot get to her.
The crew (with mobile VHF) splash there.
Another channel comes on air,
That's thick with calls on radios from everyone.

A muddy girl.
A fallen crutch.
A quickly-rising ride.
No time to spare.

She's handed to an ambulance.
The crew wade back, not finished yet.
A high-speed shout to Battersea again,
For boys on hired bikes caught climbing bridges, drunk.
Police on boats and flashing cars ashore.
I roll my eyes and wonder what we're for.

We search to Albert Bridge,
And give up there.
It's called as hoax.
We turn for home.
It's half-past-four.

10
Picnic

We meander,
Me and her.
Crossing meadows,
Rushes, shadows,
Stickelbacks and damsel flies.
Go-go-go, a heron cries.

Willow leaves.
An evening breeze.
Beneath the trees,
She looks at me.
Not kissing, yet, just drinking tea.

11
The Windrush

The greatest port on earth, *they said*
We need your hands to help, *they said*
A city paved with gold, *they said*
A city on the Thames, *they said*
Now send your money home, she said

No blacks or Irish here, *they said*
We'll keep our daughters safe, *they said*
You come to take our jobs, *they said*
You are not wanted here, *they said*
You stay, I'm coming too, she said

Dark 1950s suits and ties, too smart for driving buses,
In Sunday's best, they walk along
A riverside, ignoring white-faced glances.
Hands held together, tight and strong.

Let's stay and make it work, she said.

12
High Windows

A child on tippy-toe, begging to be lifted,
Pleads to get a view, perspective shifted.
Nervous hands. A ledge-bound boy.
He looks at boats, unzips his coat,
And darting forward appears
In mortal peril, until his quick-eyed mother grabs him back.

The problem is, from four feet high
The Thames is quite invisible.
Embanking blocks were floated here
To hold the tide, keep London dry.
For little folk (or those who drive)
There is no river here to selfie-pic
It's height you need to elevate
A view of London's waterway.

The answer to this need to see,
Is driving by, five metres tall.
A double decker, top front seat
Is one of London's finest treats.
A view that's truly VIP, and after all,
(This is the bit to make you wonder)
The seat is free,
If you're ten or under.

DANGER

13
SS Richard Montgomery

Beneath a rotten steel mast, the tide disguises TNT,
A cargo ship lies broken here,
One shoreside hikers sometimes see,
A sleeping mushroom cloud that's said to be
Beneath this peaceful estuary.

The spoils of war are sometimes spoiled by war;
These holds are rich, but not with single malt.
No Whisky Galore in Kent to cheer in black and white,
But tons of bombs and mines that might
At any moment slip, and then ignite.

Not nuclear, yet power here to match Hiroshima,
Conventional; as once blew up in Nova Scotia.
This danger posed to London ranks
So high, atop our river's ever shifting banks.

Each decade passes: divers check
The safety of this well-marked wreck.
What quaking thoughts pass through those sent 'neath deck,
To check, if any safety margin's left?

An errant ship, a pilot lost,
Or God forbid, a terrorist.
And all at once, if fuses lit
A tidal wave, like thunder-storms
Will crash along our river's shores.
Ten thousand dead, or maybe more.
Let's take the time to hope and pray,
There's life left in Montgomery.

14
Brunels

Candle wicks leave smoke beneath this river,
They flare: a gas that takes life straight from air.
36 wood-steel coffins stacked with working men,
A circled multi-storied place of work: a place to die.

Overseeing engineering, breathing damp and foetid air
A father, Marc, becomes aware as other men
That digging tunnels tortures lungs beneath a river,
And risks his project too, should all the funding die.

A bearded son waving a stovepipe hat high in the air,
Young Isambard, an accident survivor, was lucky not to die.
In front, a colonnaded tunnel crosses underneath the river.
He takes the praise, cheered by his father's men.

Victoria and Albert strolled, but not long after, worldly men
Sought ladies' solace in dark corners hidden by our river
Where penny hookers gasped for air.
And if these gentlemen were caught, they'd rather die.

A tunnel built for silk-lined ladies and for working men
Would close its decorated stairways to the air,
And see the footpath tunnel vision die.
And carries Tube trains now beneath the river.

A modern river flows, sweet evening air breezes by
A monument to tunnel men who never planned to die.

15
For a Lifeboatman

The bell has rung, and they have gone,
This pair of yellow boots, that flashed and dashed
And ran to launch an orange boat away.
By God, they saved a life today.

In wind and biting rain, these boots remain,
To carry sprinting souls away
Through dark and shoaling waters.
And keep them safe, so they can say,
They saved another life today.

These yellow boots stand empty now
And wonder how that it can be,
That after all these years at sea
They could not save your life today.

Your yellow boots stand ready now,
To reach another soul who needs to be
Restored to fear-eyed friends and family.
And hear this time a new voice say:

By God, we saved another life today.

(*For Ian Owen, 1971 – 2023. Ian served with the RNLI at Hastings and Chiswick for 27 years. He assisted 440 people, and saved 21 lives.*)

16
Vauxhall Beach

A sort of cream that doesn't fit, catches my eye,
Not just the shade, a quirky shape.
Rinsed of mud, I try to work out,
What I've found in Vauxhall's muddy ground.

A smile forms. I've caught a teapot spout,
Torn from its larger form, but obvious what it is.
I turn it in my hand, I see a dark stained chip,
That must predate whatever drama smashed it up.

How many cups of tea were poured over this chip,
To keep the stain so visible? I think
Of my cheap white teapot sat at home,
Which has a similar kink: I caught it on the kitchen sink.

I've never thrown my chipped teapot away,
Because my grandma also had a chip on hers.
When I pour a cup of morning tea
I think of her and Worthing, and a knitted cosy.

Tamesis

Kneeling on a dirty river beach,
I'm holding someone else's broken pot,
Which for moment, takes me back to reach
A fading memory of homemade treacle tart,
And steak and kidney pudding, piping hot.

How many old-chipped memories are buried here,
With stains that never wash away,
Waiting to be rinsed and rediscovered,
In a cheap bright orange bucket at low water springs today?

17
Water Eaton Eddys

A rock beneath the surface, by the bank
Forms mercury waves,
Oiled smoothing boils of water headed down,
through Oxford Town.

But here, in spate, the rock becomes a hydro engineer
Twisting streams of wolden water back uphill towards
their source;
A child left at nursery turning back to see if she can stay at
home today.

In fullest flood, quite half the river foams and roars, and
fights the urge to slip away,
A dirty teen been sent to bed, who simply will not go.
A stomping angry river, thrashing with childish tantrums.
It is a family affair, this stream, of constant mixed
emotions.

However hard the water tries, the river always wins,
And it will fall through Oxford down and head to sea.
Heavier now, and slower too.
Like mothers fighting age and gravity.

18
Belloc's Dock

It's impossible to find the tiny dock at Yarnton
Captured in rhyme by Hilaire Belloc.
Perhaps he meant to say Cassington,
Or the Oxford canal, at Kidlington Lock.

The Evenlode is spread too wide here,
A maze of Thames-ward tributaries,
Where flooding from the western wolds brings fear
To houses built to crowd the open skies.

A lonely river, invisible to those who drive,
But not to walkers, or adventurers who ride,
Particularly those on National Cycle Route 5
Between the A44 and the riverside.

A reference to ancient history
Would lift the status of this verse about a river.
A pedestrian version is more for me,
Just walking, and Googling stuff about nature.

19
Tanker Tankas

A large cargo ship
(If flammable or toxic)
Must not navigate
West of Coalhouse Point
Without an escorting tug.

And if underway
A crew member must be for'd
Ready to let go
An anchor if required
To prevent an accident.

Vessels carrying
LNG in bulk volume
Cannot navigate
Along the Princes Channel
Without prior permission.

Vessels intending
to go under Tower Bridge
Contact VTS
Thirty minutes before
Your expected ETA

20
Charlbury Floods

I know the bank drops sharply,
Muddy chutes, vole-holed and willow-rooted,
Invisible today: no tell-tale signs a river should be here.

Dark swollen water swirls above the roots of trees with
    swings where no-one plays.

New islands over there; a solitary bench
Creates a lakeside kingdom for a puzzled crow
That yesterday was feet-dry hunting
For carrion that's been washed away.

A century past, the flooding Thames brought life and
    minerals,
But now more likely human shit and diverse chemicals
That poison meadows: there's nothing sweet
About the vile liquid lapping at my feet.

21
Westminster Bridge

Not yet an old man with a famous garden,
He sits on the Embankment, staring, thinking; charcoal,
crayon.
Today he is a nobody, an amateur, a tourist, even;
But in his eyes he sees a blue-mist sky,
Framed by Gothic power, and industry in pink.
Others standing here, in darker hues,
Balanced on a pier, in silhouette.

But do they see it too?
Is there an image forming,
An impression perhaps,
Of London, and a river caught in time
By an imagination unlike mine
That years from now will redefine
What captures truth in an artist's mind.

Walking now, and measuring by hand
I cannot find his view, or not exactly.
Perhaps there is no paving stone to reach
That lines up perfectly
With Monet's eye,
Because the truth of it is not the truth of it,
It is the essence that is real, not my reality.

RNLI

22
Waterloo Sunset

You can walk this bridge from either end,
But I prefer to start down south, and walk alone
To view the life of London on this river bend;
A white bridge clad in many tons of Portland stone.

Stop.
Don't walk so fast.
There is so much of London's history cantilevered here
Between the newly-Royal National Theatre,
And the flag at the Savoy.
That bus stop, on your right, is
Where a KGB assassin thrust a poison-tipped umbrella.

And twenty years before,
The trams stopped there,
Emerging from their northern secret tunnel.
Although my mother stayed on board,
Gathering her thoughts before alighting at the County Hall,
Checking her hair for later on.
Her 50's office now holds real sharks,
And at the end, a grand hotel
Views tourists on a Ferris wheel.

Despite the City and the Eye,
The ever-changing view from here remains unchanged,
A modern Canaletto sporting crystal domes, like Wren's
spires
Rising from the City's fires,
As striking now as then.

A sunset on the other side to sing about,
And tell the time on giant clocks
That toll the chimes for bulletins, and docks
That shepherd pleasure boats.

And crossing back,
And looking east.
See down to where two ships collide, so late at night
That help was nowhere to be found,
And which is why,
If you look left,
You'll see a lifeboat floating, bright
With crews, their springs hard-coiled and standing by.

Pause here and watch commuters cross:
They have to be exhausted not to pause a moment just
to stare
At London's finest views. And some of them remember
where
They passed an old carved stone,
That names the men who cut the ribbons on this bridge
That wartime women built, yet aren't named there.

And whilst the south is of the new,
The north side gives a different view
Of wealthy homes for Somerset and Pepys
Now shared workspace for IT geeks.
Corinthia comes into sight, a glimpse of the Lyceum,
Which is where I turn and look across epochs,
From a theatre steeped in classic acts,
To a roundabout with LEDS that boast IMAX.

My mother says the same as me,
Despite the years that separate,
That if your heart is meant to be
In London, planning on a date,
There's only one place you should wait,
It's on this bridge, and don't be late.

23
Sheerness Dreams

Red canvas hangs heavy, her telltales limp.
A gentle rolling sea lifts, lazy lines dip.
A gaff spar swings and then rocks back again,
A leaden glassy sea: no clouds, no breeze, no rain.

Horizon empty, evening into night.
Tobacco from a pouch into a pipe.
They're going nowhere now, that's plain,
With forty tons below of Suffolk grain.

The drift is useful, first the flooding tide
But now the heavy anchor must be tried.
A humid night to hold against the ebb,
A thirty fathom rode to help her kedge.

Starlit, on deck a lad to stay awake,
Hot and shirtless, dozes, knowing that
If stirring whisps of breeze at morning break
He'll be the first to feel a changing sea.
The one who lights the kettle for the tea.

A bell signals a far-off shallow bank,
Sound travelling on sultry windless nights.
Above, the stars rotate, a distant light
Flickers, warning of shallows, Maplin Sands.

Tamesis

A dream is broken by a feather's touch,
An ear, a cheek, a ruffled hair enough
To shake a sleeping lad who calls to wake
The cursing crew to set up stakes
That drive a windlass round and round,
And lifts the anchor off the ground.

One knot, then two; the Old Man looks abeam,
To see if she is making headway overall,
Against the river's silent tidal stream,
Or if the hook was better, after all.

From dead astern, in pink, the dawn light breaks.
White clouds, flat-bottomed, cross a building wake.
A helpful breeze brings hints of little waves,
And fills the canvas, tensions sheets and stays.

A child at Sheerness beach is bouncing stones,
And thinking he is on his own,
Sees bold red sails two miles north,
And thinks it is a pirate ship, set forth
To capture laden Spanish galleons,
And fills his dreams with gold doubloons.

24
Greggs

We searched for hours
The person must be there:
Heard calling out for help,
But no signs anywhere.

It's called a *multi-agency response*,
Blue lights and teams that search.
Cold winter rain was howling down.
We drained our searchlights dry.

Three hours searching, maybe more,
The fire brigade turned out in force,
An ambulance with expert crews,
Tried sonar from the shore.

At 2am it's called defeat,
No happy end in sight,
We end the failed search to rest,
Uneasy in the night.

Now driving home, I stop at Gregg's
To eat the breakfast roll I've earned
With extra ketchup, coffee hot,
Relieved I find a place to sit.

I stare at other frown-faced men.
And wonder why they're here.
A sleepless night?
An early shift?

They sit, like me, alone
At grey fake marble tables,
Dead eyes looking at their maybe lists
Of things they could have done.

25
Fords

Have you ever tried to walk across the Thames?
Not proudly high on elevated bridges,
But through the brackish water step-by-step,
Tense and chilled, with arms held high,
A Saxon headed home with bales of hay.
A body set to freeze before a sudden drop.

And either side, on banks, by trees,
Eyes watch.
A startled doe that bounds too high.
Young rabbits freeze, and leverets.
They hear a danger breathing fast,
As chilly waters reach his thigh.

In darker bankside hidden groves
Lie other eyes, less keen to graze.
They see a man with arms upraised,
With focus on his slimy footing
Unaware that over there are creatures hunting
Flesh and treasures such as him.

26
Half Moon at St Margaret's

The winter moon is high above the nave.
Brighter than limed clerestory walls and flying buttresses,
Not purest white, yet brighter light than shines in pilgrim's eyes.
It's half a Moon, a vicar's hat,
A papal cap from Rome, atop a lunar pope.

Bright light, but Jesus; God, from where?
Not lit from here, because the Moon's circle
is far from whole, a shadowed part divides the lower face.
Now fully half the Moon is missing.
I fantasise a dark-faced cleric wearing what Moon is left for us to see.

If our Moon reflected earthly light, each night we'd see her full,
But Earth creates no rays, apart from bulbs creating homely incandescence,
A human light, not strong enough to bother interstellar craft.
The light we see is just our Sun, reflecting
Back at us, but ruined by our shadow.
A view obscured by our own shape.

Our bright star's light is watching us tonight, bounced
harshly on a rocky mirror,
The only dark eclipsing it is not a bishop's face beneath
a hat,
It is our darkness,
Cutting out a glint of starlight meant for other galaxies,
Reflected light caught here on limestone galleries.

A bright half-moon above the Abbey
Where queens and poets lie,
Asks questions, and I wonder why
We focus on the light we see,
And not our darkness, that more often passes by.

RNLI
RNLI
ifeboa
RNLI
RNLI
209
BUP
BUB
BUP
BUB
ROSTER E-08

27
Daily Checks

I disconnect the power from the shore,
Enjoy a moment: sunset's amber glare.
We split the jobs and I head forward,
Powering up, and getting us on air.

With comms alive, the speakers start to shout.
I flash the blues, and turn the nav lights on.
My colleague checks our mighty engines out.
Arms clear, thumbs up: I press the button down.

Four hundred horses surging into life,
Bup bub, bup bub, is that a squeaking noise?
And hearing none, I power up her sister drive.
Engage the gears, and check the engine hours.

These checks bring sense and order, every day
A random crew our rota put together.
Our list complete, we put the lifeboat back to bed,
Safe knowing that, like us, she's standing by.

We're all from different worlds tonight:
Actor, IT guru, cook and drummer,
Our radio and oil checks are just the same,
We are a team, and there's no doubt,
That if loud bells start ringing, we'll leap as one;
As though we do this every day.

Prepared for anything, we watch TV,
In fact it is a *quiet* night
(don't ever use that word!),
At dawn, we head off into diverse lives,
To real jobs based somewhere else.

Next time, I'll join a different crew.
With different moods and different skills,
But knowing that, in half an hour,
We'll head back down for daily checks,
A random gaggle dressed in yellow,
But always strolling back as one.

The Poet

Edmund Hall has served as part of the volunteer RNLI lifeboat crew on the River Thames for more than 20 years, based at the lifeboat station in Chiswick. He has lived at the other end of the Thames, next to the River Evenlode, a Thames tributary in Oxfordshire, a source of further inspiration.

A former journalist and occasional author, as well as a successful racing yachtsman, he has been writing poems inspired by the river and his work for the RNLI whilst on 12-hour shifts for many years.

The poems are often developed from single lines scribbled on a mobile phone, or ideas sent by email to himself whilst on the water patrolling on the lifeboat, or when exploring the river's banks on walks in Oxfordshire: some of these poems have taken ten years or more to reach their finished form.

Instagram @edhalluk

The Illustrator

Born and raised in London, Gary Partridge developed a passion for art at an early age. His creative journey took an unexpected turn when he joined the Coldstream Guards, with whom he served for 22 years from the Far East, to Bosnia, Northern Ireland and Iraq.

After leaving the army, Gary was diagnosed with cancer; a challenging experience which transformed his life. On successful completion of his medical treatment, Gary developed a joy for gardening while rekindling the pleasure of recording the landscapes and scenes of every day around him, in his distinctive line drawn style, working in either pencil, pen and ink or watercolour.

Gary Partridge lives in Dorset; *Tamesis* is his first commission.

Instagram @gaz1cg